AF362063

INGO BLUM

Where Is My Little Dog?

Wo ist mein kleiner Hund?

ENGLISH/GERMAN

4

Where is Bobby, my little dog?

Wo ist Bobby, mein kleiner Hund?

He is not in his doghouse.

Er ist nicht in seiner

Hundehütte.

6

He is not in his basket
with his chew bone.

Er ist nicht in seinem Korb mit

seinem Knochen.

He is not on the street
with the other dogs.

Er ist nicht auf der Straße mit
den anderen Hunden.

He likes to play
with them.

Er spielt gerne
mit ihnen.

He is not on the carousel.
Er ist nicht auf dem Karussell.

Do you see Bobby?
Siehst du Bobby?

12

He is not sitting next to
Kitty, the cat.

Er sitzt nicht neben

Kitty, der Katze.

He often sits with her
on the windowsill.

Er sitzt oft mit ihr auf

der Fensterbank.

Is he with Jimmy, the parrot?

Ist er bei Jimmy, dem Papagai?

No. He is not there either.

Nein. Dort ist er auch nicht.

Is he in the park?

Ist er im Park?

At the lake with the ducks?

Am See mit den Enten?

No, he isn't.

Nein, ist er nicht.

18

Is he on the farm?

Ist er auf dem Bauernhof?

There are many animals there.
But no dog!

Dort sind viele Tiere.

Aber kein Hund!

Look, there he is! Hooray!

Schau, da ist er! Hurra!

Bobby is lying next to Sonya, the dog lady.

Bobby liegt neben Sonya, der Hundedame.

Color the dog.

Mal den Hund aus.

More Reading and Coloring Fun

ISBN 978-1-982924-98-0

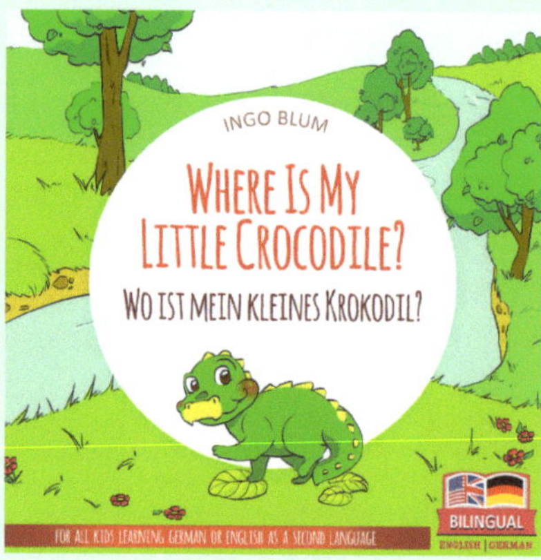

ISBN 978-1-982922-57-3

ISBN 978-1-982924-05-8

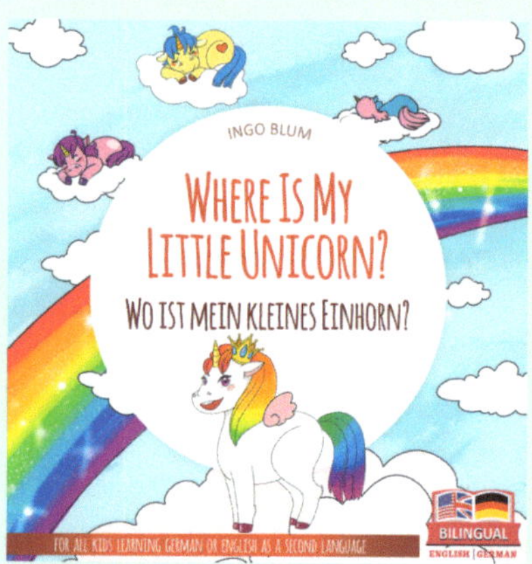

ISBN 979-8-460931-34-7

ISBN 978-1-983093-97-5

ISBN 979-8-682547-90-6

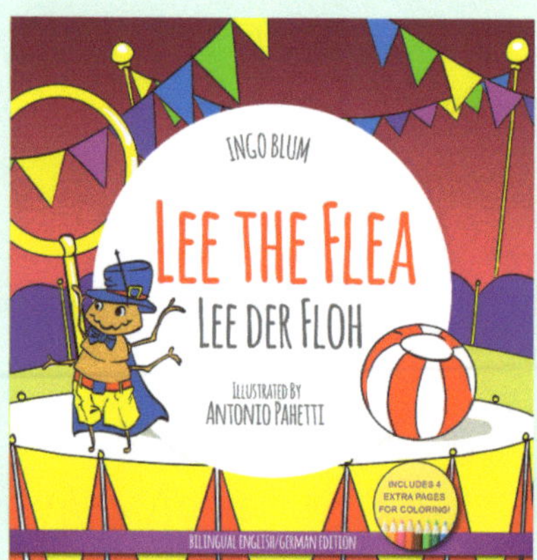

ISBN 978-1-790104-73-4

ISBN 979-8-672025-68-1

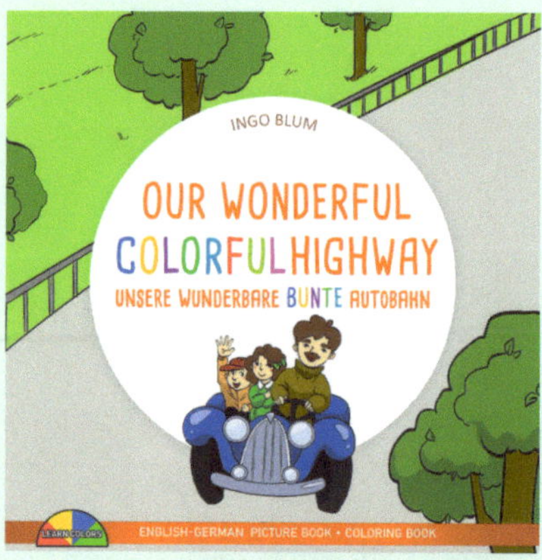

ISBN 978-1-982925-84-0